Contents

Introduction

Grades K–2 Activities

Grades 3–4 Activities

Grades 5–6 Activities

Blackline Masters

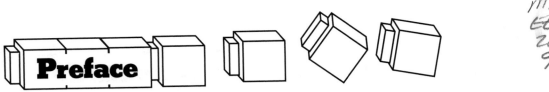

Preface

Place value is a cornerstone of the mathematics curriculum. Knowing that our number system is built on grouping by tens provides students with the foundation for understanding basic operations and later work with decimals. In the early grades, students begin to construct place-value understanding by counting, grouping, and regrouping colorful, snap-together cubes, such as PopCubes® and Snap™ Cubes.

Older children continue their study of place value and larger numbers with traditional base ten manipulatives. These are designed so that groups of ten, one hundred, and one thousand are already made and ready for trading; that is, ready to be exchanged for blocks of equal value. However, researchers have found that it is more beneficial for students to join individual objects together themselves so that they can re-count them, if necessary (Baroody 1990; Clements and McMillen 1994; Richardson 1984). In the lower grades, conservation of large numbers (the understanding that the number of objects remains the same even when they are rearranged spatially) is not fully developed, and students may need to convince themselves that the amount has not changed. If trading 10 Rods for a Flat, for instance, is introduced too soon, students may not fully grasp why they are trading.

By using Interlox™ Base Ten Blocks, students now have the option of building groups of ten and transitioning to trading when they are ready. Unit blocks can be snapped together to build Rods; Rods can be snapped together to make Flats; and Flats can be connected to make Cubes. Once students are convinced that trading does not change the amount, they can concentrate on solving problems involving grouping, rather than on making the groups themselves. Students further develop understanding of our number system with representations for 100s and 1,000s. One reason why Interlox Base Ten Blocks are such a powerful manipulative is because the dimensions of each piece are proportionate to its value. Ten Units make a Rod, and a Rod is 10 times the size of a Unit. Ten Flats make a Cube, and a Cube is 10 times the size of a Flat.

As educators, we cannot construct understanding for our students, but we can provide them with meaningful experiences involving manipulatives that will help them to observe, model, and internalize abstract mathematical concepts. Interlox Base Ten Blocks provide students with the opportunity to figure out problems for themselves, without relying on rote procedures. Moreover, they give students the chance to construct mathematical knowledge for themselves and learn that mathematics makes sense.

Astrida Cirulis, D.A.
Assistant Professor, Mathematics Education
National-Louis University, Wheaton, IL

References Cited
Baroody, Arthur J. (1990). "How and When Should Place-Value Concepts and Skills Be Taught?" *Journal for Research in Mathematics Education*, 21: 281–86.

Clements, Douglas H., and Sue McMillen (1996). "Rethinking 'Concrete' Manipulatives." *Teaching Children Mathematics*, 2(5): 270–79.

Richardson, Kathy (1984). *Developing Number Concepts Using Unifix Cubes*. Menlo Park, CA: Addison-Wesley Publishing Co.

Introducing Interlox™ Base Ten Blocks

This book contains a collection of hands-on activities and ideas you can use with Interlox Base Ten Blocks. Although the activities are written for a specific grade range, they all connect to the core of mathematics learning that is important to every K–6 student. Thus, the material in many activities can easily be adapted for students at other grade levels.

Interlox Base Ten Blocks provide a concrete, three-dimensional model of our base ten number system. They combine the visual impact of traditional base ten manipulatives with the ability to physically connect individual pieces. The smallest blocks, called Units, measure 1 cm on a side and represent ones. The long, narrow blocks, called Rods, measure 10 cm × 1 cm × 1 cm and represent tens. The flat, square blocks, known as Flats, measure 10 cm × 10 cm × 1 cm and represent hundreds. The largest blocks, called Cubes, measure 10 cm on a side and represent thousands.

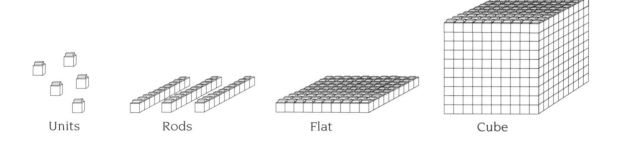

| Units | Rods | Flat | Cube |

Interlox Base Ten Blocks are ideal for providing students with ways to physically represent the concepts of place value, addition, subtraction, multiplication, and division. By building number combinations with the blocks, students ease into the concept of regrouping and are able to see the logical development of each arithmetic operation. The blocks provide a visual foundation and a better understanding of the algorithms students use when doing paper-and-pencil computation.

By letting the Cube, Flat, Rod, and Unit represent 1, 0.1, 0.01, and 0.001, respectively, students can also develop an understanding of the meaning of decimals, compare decimals, and perform basic operations with decimal numbers.

Interlox Base Ten Blocks are also ideal for developing measurement skills. The square along each face makes the blocks excellent tools for visualizing and internalizing the concepts of perimeter and surface area of structures. Counting Unit blocks in a structure can form the basis for understanding and finding volume.

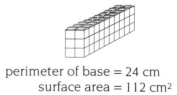

perimeter of base = 24 cm
surface area = 112 cm²
volume = 60 cm³

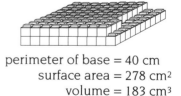

perimeter of base = 40 cm
surface area = 278 cm²
volume = 183 cm³

Teaching Place Value with Interlox Base Ten Blocks

When students initially work with Interlox Base Ten Blocks, allow them a few minutes to freely explore. Begin by questioning students about the similarities and differences they observe between the different blocks.

Hold up a Unit block and have students do the same. Introduce the name of the Unit. Tell students that the Unit has a value of 1. Next, hold up a Rod and have students do the same. Introduce the name and value of the Rod. Have students verify the value of the Rod by connecting 10 Units together and placing the structure next to a Rod to show that they are the same length. Follow the same procedure for introducing the Flat and the Cube. As students work with the blocks, continue to question them about the relationships they are uncovering.

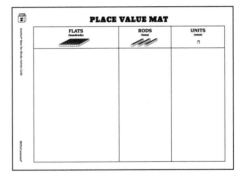

A place value mat (page 54) provides a means for students to organize their work as they explore the relationships among the blocks and determine how groups of blocks are used to represent numbers.

Students may begin by placing Units, one at a time, in the Units (ones) column on a mat. For each Unit they place, they record the number corresponding to the total number of Units placed (1, 2, 3, etc.). Students continue this process until they have accumulated 10 Units, at which point they match their 10 Units to 1 Rod and trade those Units for the Rod, which they place in the Rods (tens) column. Students continue in the same way, adding Units one at a time to the Units column and recording the totals (11, 12, 13, etc.) until it is time to trade for a second Rod, which they place in the Rods column.

When students finally come to 99, there are 9 Units and 9 Rods on the mat. Adding one more Unit forces two trades: first 10 Units for another Rod and then 10 Rods for a Flat (100). Then it is time to continue adding and recording Units and making trades as needed as students work their way through the hundreds and up to thousands. Combining the placing and trading of Rods with the act of recording numbers provides students with a connection between concrete and symbolic representations of numbers.

Each lesson has four main sections: Overview, Introducing the Activity, Thinking and Sharing, and Going Further.

Overview

This section provides a straightforward explanation of what students will be doing and why.

Introducing the Activity

The aim of this section is to help you give students the tools they will need to investigate independently. The heart of the lesson, the Student Activity, is found on the second page of each lesson. Here, rich problems and games stimulate many different problem-solving approaches and lead to a variety of solutions and strategies. These hands-on explorations have the potential for exposing students to new mathematical ideas and deepening their skills.

Thinking and Sharing

This section gives suggestions for how students can share their work and their thinking and make mathematical connections. Class charts and students' recorded work provide a springboard for discussion.

Going Further

These extension activities can be used with a class that becomes deeply involved in the primary activity or for students who finish the primary activity early. Extensions usually take the essence of the main activity and either alter or extend its parameters. They may also include a suggestion for a writing or drawing assignment.

The materials and supplies students will need to complete each activity are listed in a box on the teacher page. Specific numbers of Interlox Base Ten Blocks are suggested in this list but can be adjusted as needed. Blackline masters—provided for your convenience at the back of the book—are also referenced here. Although overhead Base Ten Blocks and the suggestion to make overhead transparencies of the blackline masters are always listed as optional, these materials are highly effective in demonstrating the use of Interlox Base Ten Blocks. As you move blocks on the screen, students can work with the same materials at their seats. Students can also use the overhead Base Ten Blocks to present their work to other members of their group or to the class.

NUMBER BUILDER

Objectives
- Use place-value vocabulary
- Identify two-digit numbers
- Communicate specific information

Materials
- Interlox Base Ten Blocks (Rods and Units)
- Large books or boxes to use as barriers
- Copy of Student Activity Sheet (page 7), one per student
- Overhead Base Ten Blocks (optional)

NCTM Curriculum Strands
Number & Operations
Problem Solving
Reasoning & Proof

Overview

Students use Interlox Base Ten Blocks to build secret numbers. Then they give clues about their secret numbers that their partners can use to try to build them.

Introducing the Activity

- Build any two-digit number with Units and Rods. Have students do the same.
- Tell students to think about what clues about the number—or about the blocks used to build it—they could give to someone who can't see the blocks.
- Call on volunteers to suggest clues. Record the clues on the board. For example, suppose you built the number 86 with 8 Rods and 6 Units. Students might give these clues.

It has 8 tens and 6 ones.	It is greater than 50.
It has 14 blocks.	It is an even number.
It is less than 100.	It is between 80 and 90.

- Ask students to identify any clues that are too general or that might be confusing.
- Try to get a consensus about which clues best describe your number.
- Distribute a copy of the Student Activity Sheet (page 7) to each student and review the directions as a class. Have students work in pairs.

Thinking and Sharing

Invite students to discuss their experiences in giving clues and in following them.

Use prompts like these to promote class discussion:
- Why were some numbers easier to build from clues than other numbers were?
- Which of your secret numbers was the easiest to give clues for? Which was the hardest? Explain.
- What kinds of clues were the most helpful?

Going Further

- Have students build their secret numbers using different numbers of blocks.
- Have students use words, numbers, and pictures to record the clues they gave for one of their secret numbers.

NUMBER BUILDER

How can you build a secret number with Interlox Base Ten Blocks and then describe it so that your partner can build it, too?

- Work with a partner. Put up a big book or box between you.
- Decide who will be the first Number Builder.
- The Number Builder:
    - ◆ secretly chooses some Rods and Units.
    - ◆ uses these blocks to build a secret number.
    - ◆ gives clues to help the partner build the secret number.
- The partner follows the clues and builds a number. Then, both partners check to see if the numbers match.
- Take turns being the Number Builder.
- Here is an example.
  These blocks show a secret number.
  See how the clues tell about the number.

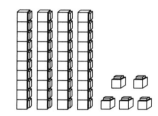

Clue 1: The number is less than 50.

Clue 2: It has 9 blocks.

Clue 3: It has more than 3 Rods but fewer than 7 Rods.

Clue 4: Its number of Units is the sum of 3 plus 2.

RACE FOR A FLAT

Objectives

- Develop understanding of place value
- Count-on by ones
- Add mentally
- Regroup Units (ones) for Rods (tens)

Materials

- Interlox Base Ten Blocks, one set per group
- Number cubes marked 1 to 6, two per group
- Copy of Student Activity Sheet (page 9), one per student
- Place Value Mat (page 54), one per pair
- Units/Rods Spinner (page 55), one per pair
- Overhead Base Ten Blocks (optional)

NCTM Curriculum Strands

Number & Operations

Overview

In this game for two pairs of students, players take turns rolling number cubes and finding the sums of the numbers rolled. They use Interlox Base Ten Blocks to represent the sums in an effort to be the first to accumulate blocks with a total value of 100.

Introducing the Activity

- Distribute a copy of the Student Activity Sheet (page 9) to each student and review the game rules as a class.
- Invite two volunteers to play part of a demonstration game with you. (You may wish to play until someone gets blocks worth 50.)
- Each player should have a place value mat. You go first.
- On your first turn, announce the sum of the digits you roll. If the sum is 10 or more, point out that you must trade 10 Units for 1 Rod.
- After your second turn, point out that the blocks on your mat are from your first and second turns combined.
- Play until each player has had several turns. Tell the rest of the class to call out "Trade!" whenever 10 Units should be traded for 1 Rod.

Thinking and Sharing

Invite students to talk about their games and describe some of the thinking they did.

Use prompts like these to promote class discussion:

- After you rolled the number cubes, how did you know how many Units to put on your mat?
- If you rolled a 5 and a 6, what would you put on your mat? Explain.
- How did you decide when to trade Units for Rods?
- What was the greatest sum you could get on one roll of two number cubes? When could rolling that sum help you win the game?

Going Further

Have pairs of teams play a variation of the game that uses just one number cube and the Units/Rods Spinner. The teams take turns rolling and spinning and putting that number of Units or Rods on their mat. Again, teams play until they can trade their Units and/or Rods for a Flat.

RACE FOR A FLAT

Play Race for a Flat! Here are the rules:

- This is a game for two teams of two players each. The object is to get enough Rods and Units to trade for a Flat worth 100.
- One team rolls two number cubes. The players find the sum of the numbers they roll and take Units to show that number. Then they put their Units on a place value mat.
- When a team gets 10 Units or more, they trade 10 Units for 1 Rod.
- Teams take turns rolling, finding the sum, putting Units on their mats, and trading Units for Rods.
- As soon as a team gets blocks worth 100 or more, they make a trade for 1 Flat. The first team to do this wins.
- Clear your mats. Now play again.
- Be ready to talk about what you did to get a Flat.

BUILD A BUG HOUSE

Objectives

- Estimate and determine the value of a group of blocks
- Compare the values of various groups of blocks

Materials

- Interlox Base Ten Blocks, one set per pair
- Copy of Student Activity Sheet (page 11), one per student
- Place Value Mat (page 54), one per pair
- Sticky notes
- Drawing paper

NCTM Curriculum Strands

Number & Operations
Problem Solving

Overview

Students build structures with Interlox Base Ten Blocks. They compare their structures by estimating the value of each structure. Then they count blocks to find the actual value of each structure and compare the actual values to their estimates.

Introducing the Activity

- Build this structure with 4 Flats. Tell students that this is your model of a doghouse.

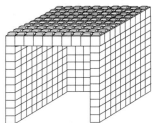

- Ask volunteers to tell what they notice about the structure.
- Elicit that the doghouse is built from 4 Flats and that the total value of the blocks that make up the doghouse is 400. Say that if doghouses had addresses, the address of this doghouse would be #400!
- Distribute a copy of the Student Activity Sheet (page 11) to each student and review the directions as a class. Have students work in pairs.

Thinking and Sharing

Encourage students to walk around the room to observe all the bug houses. Which bug house is the tallest? The shortest?

Use prompts like these to promote class discussion:

- How did you find the address of your bug house?
- When you took apart your bug house to compute its address, did you need to trade blocks? Explain.
- Do the tall bug houses have the addresses with the greatest values? Explain.
- Do the short bug houses have the addresses with the least values? Explain.

Going Further

- Challenge students to build a bug house with a particular address.
- Have students draw a bug that could live in one of their bug houses. Then have them tell why that house would make a good home for the bug.

BUILD A BUG HOUSE

How can you use Interlox Base Ten Blocks to build a bug house?

- Work with a partner. Each of you take up to 16 blocks. You may take any combination of Flats, Rods, and Units.

- Use all your blocks to build a bug house.

- Compare bug houses. Guess the value of each. The value is also the "address" of the bug house. Try to count the blocks without touching them to guess the address.

- Write the address on a sticky note. Carefully stick the address on the house.

- Draw a picture of your bug house.

- Now take your bug house apart. Put the blocks on a place value mat.

- Find the value of the blocks on the mat. See if you guessed the address correctly.

- Do the activity again. This time, try to build a better bug house—maybe even a bigger bug house!

- Don't take your bug house apart. Leave it out where everyone can see it.

SUM IT UP!

Objectives

- Reinforce number recognition
- Use counting and addition skills
- Record the sum of two-digit numbers

Materials

- Interlox Base Ten Blocks, one set per group
- Copy of Student Activity Sheet (page 13), one per student
- Sum It Up! worksheet (page 56), one or two per group
- Overhead Base Ten Blocks and/or Sum It Up! worksheet transparency (optional)

NCTM Curriculum Strands

Number & Operations
Problem Solving
Communication

Overview

Students use Interlox Base Ten Blocks to model the sum of two addends. Then they find ways to model the same sum with different pairs of addends.

Introducing the Activity

- Display 1 Rod and 8 Units and have students do the same.
- Count the blocks aloud with the class to establish that they model the number 18.
- Invite a volunteer to separate the blocks into two groups and name the value of each, saying, for example, "This group has 12, and that group has 6."
- Now ask the volunteer to push the two groups together. Record an addition sentence for this action on the board, such as 12 + 6 = 18. (Make sure that students know the meanings of the terms *addend* and *sum*.)
- Invite another volunteer to use 18 Units to make and identify two different groups.
- Ask another volunteer to combine these two groups and record an addition sentence for this action, such as 9 + 9 = 18. Elicit that the addition sentences on the board have the same sum, even though they have different addends.
- Mix all the blocks together again. Invite other students to each make two different groups from the 18 and then put their groups together and write an addition sentence to record what they did.
- Reiterate that all students' addition sentences have the same sum, 18.
- Distribute a copy of the Student Activity Sheet (page 13) to each student and review the directions as a class. Have students work in groups of three.

Thinking and Sharing

Invite groups to exchange worksheets and then discuss among themselves how the other groups built the addends for their sum.

Use prompts like these to promote class discussion:

- How were your number sentences alike? How were they different?
- Did your group find all the possible ways to show your sum? How do you know?
- When it was your turn to build two addends for the sum, what did you think about first?
- Which job did you like better, building two addends for your sum, drawing the blocks for someone else's addends, or writing the addition sentence? Why?

Going Further

Have students repeat the activity, but this time have them find three addends for their group's original sum.

SUM IT UP!

How many different ways can you show the same sum with Interlox Base Ten Blocks?

- Working in a group of three, think of a two-digit number.
- Build your number with Rods and Units. Put your blocks in the box at the top of the worksheet.
- Pretend that your number is a sum. Write your sum on the worksheet.
- Show six or more different ways to make your sum. Here's how:
  - ◆ Decide which of you will use your Rods and Units to build two groups of addends.
  - ◆ Talk about the value of the blocks for each addend.
  - ◆ Decide which of you will draw pictures of the blocks, one group in each box.
  - ◆ Decide which of you will record an addition sentence for what you did.
  - ◆ Use blocks to check your work.

- Take turns building two different addends. Take turns drawing and recording, too.
- Compare your addition sentences. Make sure the sums are all the same. Check that the pairs of addends are different.
- Leave your worksheet out so that others can see it.
- Be ready to talk about how you made your pairs of addends.

WHAT'S THE DIFFERENCE?

Objectives

- Explore the meaning of subtraction
- Record basic subtraction facts

Materials

- Interlox Base Ten Blocks, one set per pair
- Counters of two different colors, one of each color per pair
- Index cards
- Copy of Student Activity Sheet (page 15), one per student
- What's the Difference? Game Board (page 57), one per pair
- One or Two Spinner (page 58), one per pair
- Overhead Base Ten Blocks and/or What's the Difference? Game Board transparency (optional)

NCTM Curriculum Strands

Number & Operations
Communication

Overview

In this game for two players, students use Interlox Base Ten Blocks to find given differences as they move around a game board.

Introducing the Activity

- Ask students what the answer to an addition problem is called.
- Explain that just as "sum" is the term for the answer to an addition problem, "difference" is the term for the answer to a subtraction problem.
- Ask someone to name a number between 0 and 10. Model the suggested number with Units.
- Write an open subtraction sentence on the board (either horizontally or vertically) with the suggested number as the difference. For example, if a student named 7, you would write ___ – ___ = 7.
- Call for a pair of numbers for which 7 could be the difference.
- Have a volunteer put two more groups of Units with the model to show how taking away one group of Units from the other group of Units results in the difference, in this case, 7. After checking the student's work, allow him or her to record it by completing the open subtraction sentence.
- Call on other volunteers to model and record subtraction sentences that have the same difference.
- Distribute a copy of the Student Activity Sheet (page 15) to each student and review the directions as a class. Have students work in pairs.

Thinking and Sharing

Invite students to talk about their games and describe their thinking.

Use prompts like these to promote class discussion:

- What was difficult about this activity? What was easy?
- How did you go about finding a subtraction fact for a difference?
- Did you ever think of more than one fact for a difference? If so, what was the difference? What facts did you think of? How did you decide which fact to use?
- Did you show and write the same fact more than once? Was there any other fact that you could have written?

Going Further

Have students play a simpler version of this game. Tell students that the number they land on is the difference that remains when they subtract a mystery number from 10. Record an open subtraction sentence for this as: 10 – (mystery number) = (landing number). As students play, have them first record each number they land on as the difference for the open sentence and then complete the sentence by finding the mystery number.

WHAT'S THE DIFFERENCE?

Play What's the Difference? Here are the rules:

- Get counters so that you and your partner can move from START to FINISH on the game board. Take turns spinning the spinner.

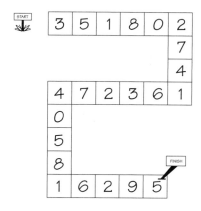

- On your turn, spin the spinner. Move one or two spaces to match your spin.

- The number you land on is the difference for a subtraction fact. Use Units to find a subtraction fact that has this difference. Record your subtraction fact on an index card. Have your partner check your work.

- Continue playing until someone gets to FINISH.

FEED THE BIRDS

Objectives

- Represent the commutative property of addition
- Explore the inverse relationship of addition and subtraction

Materials

- Interlox Base Ten Units (20 per pair) and Rods (10 per pair)
- Copy of Student Activity Sheet (page 17), one per student
- Feed the Birds workmat (page 59), one per student
- Overhead Base Ten Blocks and/or Feed the Birds workmat transparency (optional)

NCTM Curriculum Strands

Number & Operations
Reasoning & Proof

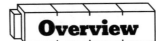

Overview

Students use Interlox Base Ten Units to model two addition facts and two related subtraction facts.

Introducing the Activity

- Invite three students to the front of the classroom. Have them count themselves aloud.
- Call up two more students. Tell them to count themselves aloud.
- Record the action by writing this addition fact on the board: 3 + 2 = 5. Then have everyone return to their seats.
- Repeat the process, this time calling up two students first and then having three students join them. Record this on the board: 2 + 3 = 5.
- Establish that five students are at the front of the room. Then ask two of the students to return to their seats. Record the subtraction fact for this action: 5 − 2 = 3.
- Now ask the two children who just sat down to rejoin the three students at the front of the room. Then tell the three students to return to their seats.
- Have a volunteer come to the board to record this action: 5 − 3 = 2.
- Lead a discussion about how the four number facts on the board are alike in some ways and different in others.
- Distribute a copy of the Student Activity Sheet (page 17) to each student and review the directions as a class. Have students work in pairs.

Thinking and Sharing

Call on pairs to tell how many birds they flew to their bird feeder. Have them come up to the board and record the addition and subtraction stories they identified for their two flocks of birds.

Use prompts like these to promote class discussion:

- How are your addition stories like your subtraction stories? How are they different from your subtraction stories?
- Why could you write two addition stories for the same two flocks of birds?
- Why could you write two subtraction stories that start with the same number of birds?

Going Further

Have children draw birds on the perches of the bird feeder to represent the two flocks of birds that they and their partner "flew" to their feeder.

FEED THE BIRDS

In how many different ways can you use Interlox Base Ten Blocks to "feed the birds"?

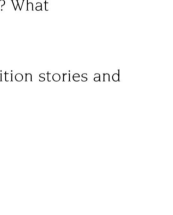

- Work with a partner. Pretend that Unit blocks are birds. Get ready to make some "birds" fly to a bird feeder.

- Each of you take some birds. Fly your birds to one perch on a bird feeder that looks like this. (Your partner should fly birds to the other perch.)

- How many birds did you fly to the perch? How many did your partner fly?

- How many birds are eating at the feeder now? Record the addition fact to tell this story.

- What if each of you flew your birds so that they landed on the other perch? Record the addition fact that tells about this.

- Now your birds have had enough to eat. Make your birds fly away. (Your partner's birds should stay.) Record a subtraction fact that tells about this.

- What if your partner's birds flew away first and your birds stayed? What subtraction fact could you write then? Write it.

- Make all the birds fly away.

- Fly two more flocks of birds to the feeder. Write and tell two addition stories and two subtraction stories about these birds.

WAYS TO PAY

Objectives
- Model three-digit numbers
- Build addition skills
- Understand the relationship between pennies, dimes, and dollars.

Materials
- Interlox Base Ten Blocks, one set per pair
- Copy of Student Activity Sheet (page 19), one per student
- Place Value Mat (page 54), one per student
- What Will You Buy? worksheet (page 60), one per pair
- Overhead Base Ten Blocks (optional)

NCTM Curriculum Strands
Number & Operations
Measurement

Overview

Using Base Ten Units, Rods, and Flats to represent pennies, dimes, and dollars respectively, students find two or more block combinations with which to pay for something they want to buy.

Introducing the Activity

- Model a three-digit number on a place value mat using Rods and Units only. For example, display 14 Rods and 5 Units.
- Call on a volunteer to identify the number.
- Ask students to model the number 145 on their own mats in a different way. For example, students are likely to display 1 Flat, 4 Rods, and 5 Units. Elicit that by displaying the number 145 in this way they used fewer blocks than you did.
- Write the number 145 on the board. Then insert a dollar sign and decimal point.
- Point to the amount on the board and tell students to pretend that Units are pennies. Elicit that 145 pennies have the same value as $1.45.
- Distribute a copy of the Student Activity Sheet (page 19) to each student and review the directions as a class. Have students work in pairs.

Thinking and Sharing

Cut apart a What Will You Buy? worksheet. Tape the 12 pictured items on the board. Have pairs of students post their "ways to pay" for each item.

Use prompts like these to promote class discussion:
- How many ways did you find to pay for _____? Tell about each way.
- Which way to pay for _____ used the least number of blocks? Which way used the greatest number of blocks?

Going Further

Bring supermarket sale flyers or newspaper advertisements to class. Allow students to pick out a sale item that they would like to buy. Tell them to imagine that they could pay for that item with Interlox Base Ten Blocks. Have them describe how they would pay for that item with the least number of blocks.

WAYS TO PAY

How can you show a way to pay for something with Interlox Base Ten Blocks?

- Work with a partner. Pretend that the blocks are different kinds of money. Here's what block money is worth:

  1 Unit = 1 penny, or 1¢

  1 Rod = 1 dime, or 10¢

  1 Flat = 1 dollar, or $1.00, or 100¢

- Look at the worksheet to see all the things you can buy. Together decide on something to buy.

- Put blocks on a place value mat to show a way to pay for what you buy.

- Your partner should put blocks on another place value mat to show a different way to pay for the same things.

- Are there other ways to pay for this with blocks? Record all the ways.

- Now decide on something else to buy. Take turns being first to show a way to pay.

MAKING RECTANGLES

Objectives

- Understand the attributes of rectangles
- Realize that a rectangle's orientation does not affect its size or shape
- Explore the concept of area

Materials

- Interlox Base Ten Blocks, one set per pair
- Copy of Student Activity Sheet (page 21), one per student
- Base Ten Block Grid Paper (page 61), one per student
- Overhead Base Ten Blocks (optional)

NCTM Curriculum Strands

Number & Operations
Geometry
Measurement

Overview

Students try to make as many different rectangles as possible using 12 Unit blocks.

Introducing the Activity

- Ask students to tell what they know about rectangles.
- Draw a rectangle on the board. Count the sides and the corners aloud with the class.
- Tell students to each use 6 Units to form a rectangle. Then guide students to count the Units to confirm that there are six.
- Call on a volunteer to describe his or her rectangle.
- Ask someone else to describe a rectangle that looks different, even though it has the same number of rows and the same number of Units in each row as the first volunteer's rectangle.
- Be sure that students understand that two rectangles can be the same, even though they are oriented differently.
- Distribute a copy of the Student Activity Sheet (page 21) to each student and review the directions as a class. Have students work in pairs.

Thinking and Sharing

Invite one pair to display the recording they made of one of their rectangles and describe them while the other students check to see if they recorded the same ones. Ask another pair to display a different 12-Unit rectangle. Continue until all possible 12-Unit rectangles are on display.

Use prompts like these to promote class discussion:

- How many different 12-Unit rectangles did you find?
- How are your rectangles the same? How are they different?
- How could you turn one of your rectangles to show a different rectangle?
- How can you describe a rectangle by its number of rows and the number of units in each row?

Going Further

- Have students use words, numbers, and pictures to tell how some rectangles made with 12 blocks are alike and how some are different.
- Have pairs repeat the activity using 16 Units to make rectangles.

MAKING RECTANGLES

How many different rectangles can you make using 12 Unit blocks?

- Work with a partner. Get ready to make rectangles using Unit blocks.
- Count out 12 Units.
- Use all 12 Units to make a rectangle.
- Talk about this rectangle with your partner.
- Record your rectangle on grid paper.
- Have your partner record it in a different way.
- Use the same 12 Units to make a different rectangle. Record it in two ways.
- Keep on making and recording 12-Unit rectangles until you have made as many as you can.
- Be ready to talk about your work.

RIDDLE ME THIS

Overview

Students model a number using Interlox Base Ten Blocks. They create clues to help others guess the number and how they modeled it.

Introducing the Activity

- Prepare a "riddle bag" by putting 1 Flat, 3 Rods, and 2 Units into a paper bag.
- Display the bag. Tell students that you will give them clues to help them answer the riddle "Which blocks are in this bag and what number do they model?"
- Write the following clues on the board:

    There are 6 blocks in the bag.

    They model a number that is greater than 100 and less than 200.

    There are exactly 3 Rods in the bag.

- Have students use blocks to model the solution.
- When they are ready, have students display their solutions. Then reveal the contents of the riddle bag so they can check their work.
- Ask students to tell how they used each clue to help them solve the riddle.
- Discuss what constitutes a good clue. Then point out that a good set of clues leads to just one solution.
- Distribute a copy of the Student Activity Sheet (page 23) to each student and review the directions as a class. Have students work in pairs.

Thinking and Sharing

Invite students to talk about how they wrote and tested their own clues and how they followed the other pair's clues.

Use prompts like these to promote class discussion:
- How did you decide what clues to use?
- What words did you use to describe your number?
- Was it easier to write clues or to follow them? Why?
- Does the order of the clues in a set matter?
- Did you have to use all the clues to solve the riddle?

Going Further

Have students use blocks to show one number in two different ways. Tell them that, for example, they can represent the number 21 either with 2 Rods and 1 Unit or with 1 Rod and 11 Units. Once they have decided on the two ways, have students write a set of clues for each way of modeling their number.

RIDDLE ME THIS

How would you write a set of clues about Interlox Base Ten Blocks for a number riddle?

- Work with a partner. Use Interlox Base Ten Blocks to show any two-digit or three-digit number.

- Examine your blocks and take turns describing the number to each other in different ways.

- Talk about clues that you could give about your blocks to help others answer the riddle "Which blocks are in this bag and what number do they model?"

- Write down your best clues on a card.

- Now test your clues. Are you sure that others could use them to solve the riddle? Do you need to change any clues? Do you need to add any clues?

- When you are satisfied with your clues, do this.
    - ◆ Put your blocks into a bag.
    - ◆ Close the bag.
    - ◆ Clip the card to the bag.

- Exchange riddle bags with another pair. Follow the other pair's clues to solve the riddle. Use blocks to model the solution. Then look into the bag to check.

PLACE IT!

Objectives
- Do mental computation
- Develop strategic thinking skills

Materials
- Interlox Base Ten Blocks, one set per group
- Number Cube marked 1 to 6, two per group
- Copy of Student Activity Sheet (page 25), one per student
- Put-in-Place Mats (page 62), one per student
- Overhead Base Ten Blocks and/or Put-in-Place Mat transparency (optional)

NCTM Curriculum Strands
Number & Operations
Reasoning & Proof

Overview

In this game for two to four players, students take turns rolling number cubes and then making a two-digit number with Units and Rods in an effort to be the one who accumulates blocks with the total value closest to 100 without going over.

Introducing the Activity

- Tell students that you rolled a pair of number cubes and the number 6 and the number 2 came up. Write 6 on the board. Then write 2 below the 6.
- Ask a volunteer to come to the board and rewrite these digits as a two-digit number. Have another volunteer write the same digits as a different two-digit number.
- Invite several pairs of students to roll two number cubes and then name two different two-digit numbers for each roll.
- Distribute a copy of the Student Activity Sheet (page 25) to each student. Explain the game rules. Be sure that students understand the conditions for scoring a rejected throw. Point out that once blocks are placed on a turn they may not be changed or rejected.
- Demonstrate by playing a partial game of Place It! with a volunteer.

Thinking and Sharing

Invite students to talk about their games and describe some of the thinking they did.

Use prompts like these to promote class discussion:
- How did you decide which two-digit number to use on each roll?
- Were you every sorry that you didn't use the other number you rolled? Explain.
- Did you ever decide to reject a throw? If so, tell why.
- How did you decide whose sum was closest to 100?
- Do you have a strategy for winning this game? Do you think that it will always work? Explain.

Going Further

- Have students play another game of Place It!, this time playing so that the winner is the one whose total is closest to 100 even if it goes above 100.
- Have students record the numbers that they used for one game. Suggest that they look at this data and write about how they might have changed one number or another in order to get closer to 100.

PLACE IT!

Play Place It! Here are the rules:

- This is a game for two to four players. The object is to get blocks that have a total value close to 100 without going over.

- A player rolls the number cubes and decides how to read the digits that come up as a two-digit number. The player takes Units and Rods to show that number and places the blocks on a Put-in-Place Mat.

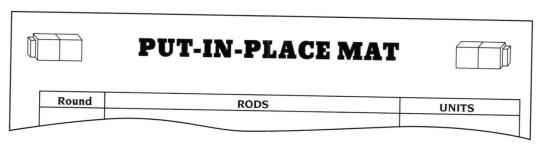

Round	RODS	UNITS

- Each of the other players takes a turn rolling the number cubes, deciding on a two-digit number, and placing blocks on his or her mat to show the number.

- Play continues for a total of five rounds.

- A player may reject any one throw if it seems that either of the two-digit numbers would add too much to his or her sum. Each player may do this only once during a game. The player must count a rejected throw as one of the five rounds by giving it a score of 0 for the round.

- After five rounds, players find the total values of their blocks and record them. Whoever gets closest to 100 without going over is the winner.

CLEAR THE MAT!

Objectives
- Use estimation skills
- Use subtraction
- Develop strategic thinking skills

Materials
- Interlox Base Ten Blocks, one set per pair
- Number cubes marked 1 to 6, two per pair
- Copy of Student Activity Sheet (page 27), one per student
- Place Value Mat (page 54), one per pair
- Overhead Base Ten Blocks (optional)

NCTM Curriculum Strands
Number & Operations
Problem Solving

 **Overview**

In this game for teams of two, students roll a number cube to determine the value of the blocks to remove from their place value mats. They look for a strategy to be the first team to remove all the blocks from their mat.

Introducing the Activity

- Show students a place value mat with 1 Flat in the Flats (hundreds) column. Elicit that the Flat represents one hundred, or 100 Units.
- Ask a volunteer to write any two-digit number on the board.
- Tell students to think about how they can take blocks equal in value to that number from the Flat on the mat.
- Establish that, in order to subtract, they would have to trade—1 Flat for 10 Rods and then, if necessary, 1 Rod for 10 Units.
- Have someone do the trading, taking away the blocks for the two-digit number and then announcing the difference, or how much of the hundred is left.
- Record the action by writing the corresponding subtraction example on the board.
- Distribute a copy of the Student Activity Sheet (page 27) to each student and review the directions as a class. Have students work in pairs.

Thinking and Sharing

Invite students to talk about their games and describe some of the thinking they did.

Use prompts like these to promote class discussion:
- On each roll, how did you decide which two-digit number to make?
- What kind of trading did you have to do in order to subtract?
- Which subtractions were the easiest to do? Explain.
- What was the greatest number you could subtract on any one turn? What was the least number?

 **Going Further**

Have teams play Fill the Mat!, a version of the game based on addition. Teams start with empty mats and take turns rolling the number cubes. The first team to fill the mat with blocks having a total value of 300 wins the game.

CLEAR THE MAT!

Play Clear the Mat! Here are the rules:

- This is a game for two to four teams of two players each. The object is to be the first team to remove all the blocks from their place value mat.

- Each team starts with 3 Flats on their mat.

- Teams take turns rolling the number cubes and using the numbers rolled to make a two-digit number. (For example, a team that rolls a 3 and a 5 could make either 35 or 53.) One team member says the number and takes blocks with that value off the mat. The other team member writes the subtraction sentence. The other teams help check their work.

- A team loses a turn if
    - they make a mistake subtracting, or
    - each of the numbers they can make is greater than the value of the blocks left on their mat.

- On any turn, if a team decides to subtract just a few blocks, they may choose to roll just one number cube.

- Play continues until one team rolls the exact amount left on their mat. Then they clear their mat and win the game!

BUILDING BOXES

Objectives
- Explore volume
- Discover that rectangular prisms with different dimensions can have the same volume
- Use spatial reasoning

Materials
- Interlox Base Ten Blocks, 1 Flat and at least 8 Rods per pair
- Small closed box
- Copy of Student Activity Sheet (page 29), one per student

NCTM Curriculum Strands
Number & Operations
Geometry
Measurement

 **Overview**

Students build as many different rectangular prisms as they can from 8 Rods.

 **Introducing the Activity**

- Display a small closed box. Establish that each side of the box is a rectangle—a shape that has four square corners and two equal lengths and widths.
- Elicit that the entire box has eight square corners and the dimensions of length, width, and height.
- Hold up a Flat and describe it as a kind of box. Allow students to examine the Flat and give its dimensions. (Be sure that they understand that the Flat has a length of 10 Units, a width of 10 Units, and a height of 1 Unit.)
- Ask students how many cubes make up the Flat.
- Tell students that another name for a figure shaped like a box is *rectangular prism*. Explain that the number of cubic units that make up a box is called the *volume* of the box.
- Distribute a copy of the Student Activity Sheet (page 29) to each student and review the directions as a class. Have students work in pairs.

 **Thinking and Sharing**

Create a class chart on the board. Discuss students' charted data.

DIMENSIONS OF BOX				CUBIC UNITS IN BOX
Layers	Length	Width	Height	Volume
1	10	8	1	80
1	20	4	1	80
1	40	2	1	80
1	80	1	1	80
2	20	2	2	80
2	10	4	2	80

Use prompts like these to promote class discussion:
- How did you go about building your boxes?
- What did you do to find the length, width, and height of each box?
- Did you ever think that two boxes were different but later find that they were really the same? Explain.
- What patterns do you see in the chart?
- How can you use the dimensions of any box to find the total number of cubic units in that box?

 **Going Further**

Ask students to use Rods to build several different boxes, each with a volume of 200 cubic units.

BUILDING BOXES

How many different boxes can you make from the same number of Rods?

- Work with a partner. Talk about ways of making a box using only Rods.
- Now build all the different boxes you can make from 8 Rods. You may put the Rods in one layer or in more than one layer.
- As you work, record on the chart the length, width, and height of each box.
- Look for patterns in your chart.

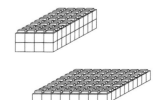

DIMENSIONS OF BOX				CUBIC UNITS IN BOX
Layers	**Length**	**Width**	**Height**	**Volume**

EVEN IT UP!

Objectives

- View division as making equal shares
- Develop an understanding of the meaning of average

Materials

- Interlox Base Ten Blocks, one set per group
- Small paper bags, 2 per group: one labeled *Rods* that contains three slips of paper marked 1, 2, and 3 and one labeled *Units*, that contains nine slips of paper marked 1–9
- Copy of Student Activity Sheet (page 31), one per student
- Overhead Base Ten Blocks (optional)

NCTM Curriculum Strands

Number & Operations
Problem Solving
Reasoning & Proof

Overview

Students pick slips of paper that indicate which two-digit numbers to model with blocks. Then they work in a group to figure out ways to share all their blocks equally.

Introducing the Activity

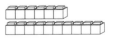

- Display a row of 6 Units. Form another row of blocks by placing 1 Rod below the Units, aligning the rows at one end. Have students copy this.
- Ask students how they can make the two rows equal in number.
- Elicit that one way to start is by trading the Rod for 10 Units.
- Have students share their strategies for "evening up" the rows.
- After students have made two rows of 8 Units, explain that by making the rows equal, they are showing that 8 is the average of 6 and 10.
- Tell students to rearrange their 16 Units into a row of 12 and a row of 4. Then ask them to find the number that is the average of 12 and 4.
- Discuss why it is possible for one number to be the average of more than one set of numbers.
- Distribute a copy of the Student Activity Sheet (page 31) to each student and review the directions as a class. Have students work in groups of three.

Thinking and Sharing

Have groups list the numbers they started with, the total value of their blocks, and the value of each share (the average). Compile their findings in a class chart like this one.

	Value of Numbers Picked	Total Value of Each Group's Blocks	Value of Each Share (Average)
Sue	12 ⎤		
Robert	18 ⎬	51	17
Lee	21 ⎦		

Use prompts like these to promote class discussion:

- What number did each person in your group start with?
- How did you go about finding the equal shares?
- Did you have to make trades? Did you rearrange the blocks in some other way? Explain.
- If you had blocks that you couldn't share three ways, what did you do? How do you think the extras would affect the average?

Going Further

Have students add two more Units to each of their starting numbers and then predict how these additions might affect the average.

EVEN IT UP!

How can you share Interlox Base Ten Blocks equally so that everyone has blocks with the same value?

- Work in a group of three. Get a bag marked *Rods* and a bag marked *Units*.
- Take turns picking. When it is your turn:
    - ◆ Pick a slip of paper from the Rods bag. Take blocks for that many Rods.
    - ◆ Return the slip to the Rods bag.
- Then, pick a slip from the Units bag. Take blocks for that many Units.
- Return the slip to the Units bag.
- Find the total value of the Rods and Units you picked. Write down the number.
- Have each group member show his or her blocks and tell the number.
- Find a way to share all the blocks that everyone picked so that you each get blocks with the same value. Decide on a way to record what you did.
- Now, do the activity again. This time, work in a group of four or five.

IT'S IN THE BAG

Objectives

- View division as making equal shares
- Predict outcomes
- Look for patterns in division problems
- Discover that multiplication is the inverse of division

Materials

- Interlox Base Ten Blocks, one set per group
- Small paper bag marked with a letter and filled with a collection of Flats and Rods representing an amount such as 15, 18, 20, 24, 25, 26, 27, 28, 30, and 36; one per group
- Copy of Student Activity Sheet (page 33), one per student
- Overhead Base Ten Blocks (optional)

NCTM Curriculum Strands

Number & Operations

Overview

Students work in groups to determine whether or not a collection of blocks can be shared equally among them with no remainder.

Introducing the Activity

- Display 1 Rod and 2 Units. Establish that the value of these blocks is 12.
- Call on two volunteers. Ask them what they can do to share the blocks so that they each get blocks of equal value.
- After students show how to trade the Rod for 10 Units, they should distribute the 12 Units equally so that each has 6 of them.
- Take the 6 Units back from each student and say that you are going to "trade the blocks back" for the Rod and 2 Units.
- Now ask five volunteers to show how they can share 1 Rod and 2 Units equally. After they make five shares of two, acknowledge that 2 Units remain. This is the *remainder*.
- Distribute a copy of the Student Activity Sheet (page 33) to each student and review the directions as a class. Have students work in groups of five.

Thinking and Sharing

After students have worked with two or more bags of blocks, ask volunteers from different groups to share some of their discoveries. Set up a class chart with headings like these to accommodate students' data.

Letter on Bag	Value of Blocks in Bag	Number of Students Sharing	Will there be leftovers?	Number of Units in Each Share	Number of Blocks Left Over

Use prompts like these to promote class discussion:

- When were you able to predict accurately that you would be able to share the blocks equally with no remainder? Explain.
- Which bags of blocks could be shared the greatest number of ways with no remainder? Why do you think this is so?
- Which bags of blocks could be shared the least number of ways? Why do you think this is so?
- What patterns do you see in your data?

Going Further

Provide students with bags that contain Flats as well as Rods and Units. Have them make two equal shares of the contents, first predicting whether or not there will be a remainder.

 **Name** _____

 **Date** _____

IT'S IN THE BAG

When you make equal shares of Interlox Base Ten Blocks, will there be any remainder?

- Work with a group of five. Get a bag of blocks. Empty the blocks from the bag.
- Find the value of the blocks. Record the letter of the bag and the total value of the blocks.
- Predict whether or not two of you can share the blocks equally with no remainder.
- Two of you should share the blocks equally. Record how many blocks each of you gets. Record the number of the remainder, if any.
- Put all the blocks together again.
- Now share the same blocks equally among three of you, then among four of you, then among five of you. Each time, first predict whether or not there will be a remainder. Then record and share your findings.
- Return all the blocks to the bag. Close the bag.
- Trade bags with another group. Repeat the activity using your new bag.

	Letter on Bag	Value of Blocks in Bag	Number of Students Sharing	Will there be leftovers?	Number of Units in Each Share	Number of Blocks Left Over
Bag 1			2			
			3			
			4			
			5			
Bag 2			2			
			3			
			4			
			5			

DECIMAL DECISIONS

Objectives

- Develop an understanding of decimal place value
- Model decimal amounts
- Compare the relative values of tenths and hundredths
- Add decimal amounts

Materials

- Interlox Base Ten Blocks, one set per pair
- Number cubes marked 1 to 6, one per pair
- Copy of Student Activity Sheet (page 35), one per student

NCTM Curriculum Strands

Number & Operations

 **Overview**

Students use blocks to model a "major decimal." Then they decide how to model a "minor decimal," a decimal whose value is less than that of the major decimal.

Introducing the Activity

- Display a Flat and have students do the same. Tell students to snap together 10 Rods. Elicit that 10 Rods are equal to 1 Flat.
- Elicit that if a Flat has the value of 1, then each Rod has the value of one-tenth (1/10) of 1. Write 0.1 on the board and explain that this is the decimal form of the fraction one-tenth.
- Then write 0.3. Tell students to use their blocks to show three-tenths.
- Display a Unit; ask how many Units would have to be snapped together to make 1 Flat. Elicit that 100 Units are equal to 1 Flat.
- Elicit that if a Flat has the value of 1, then each Unit has the value of one-hundredth (1/100) of 1. Write 0.01 on the board. Explain that this is the way to write the fraction one-hundredth as a decimal.
- Now write 0.14. Challenge students to use their blocks to show fourteen-hundredths. Establish that there are two ways to do this—with 1 Rod and 4 Units and with 14 Units.
- Distribute a copy of the Student Activity Sheet (page 35) to each student and review the directions as a class. Have students work in pairs.

Thinking and Sharing

Invite students to identify their major decimals and to tell how they modeled their minor decimals. Have pairs share the number sentences they wrote to compare the decimals.

Use prompts like these to promote class discussion:

- What is the greatest major decimal you can model? The least?
- How did you figure out the value of your major decimal?
- How did you model your minor decimal?
- Were you always able to model a minor decimal? Explain.
- How did you compare your decimals? How else could you compare?

 **Going Further**

Have students do the activity two more times, but instead of having them compare each pair of major and minor decimals, have them record and order the four decimals they model, from least to greatest.

DECIMAL DECISIONS

How can you use Interlox Base Ten Blocks to show a decimal that is worth less than a "major decimal"?

- Work with a partner. Put a Flat between you. Your Flat has the value of 1.
- Whoever goes first models a *major decimal*. Here's how:
    - ◆ Roll a number cube. Take Rods to match the number rolled. Record the value of the Rods as a number of tenths.
    - ◆ Roll again. Take Units to match the number rolled. Record their value as hundredths.
    - ◆ Combine the blocks. Find the sum they represent. Write the sum in decimal form. (This is your major decimal.)

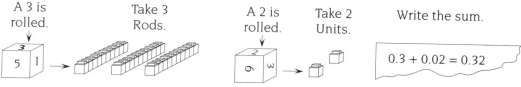

A 3 is rolled. → Take 3 Rods. → A 2 is rolled. → Take 2 Units. → Write the sum.
0.3 + 0.02 = 0.32

- Whoever goes second models a *minor decimal* this way:
    - ◆ Roll the number cube. What digit did you roll? Model it with Rods (tenths) or Units (hundredths) or with both Rods and Units. You must represent a sum whose value is *less than* the value of the major decimal.
    - ◆ Record the value of your minor decimal.

0.06   0.32 > 0.06

- Write a number sentence that compares the two decimals.
- Repeat the activity several times. Take turns going first.

SCHOOL SIZES

Objectives

- Explore the concept of area
- Use estimation skills
- Use spatial reasoning

Materials

- Interlox Base Ten Blocks, one set per pair
- Markers
- Copy of Student Activity Sheet (page 37), one per student
- Base Ten Block Grid Paper (page 61), one per student
- School Floor Plans worksheet (page 63), one per pair

NCTM Curriculum Strands

Geometry
Number & Operations
Measurement

 **Overview**

Students estimate the area of irregular polygons. Then they use blocks to determine the actual area of each.

Introducing the Activity

- Use a marker to write the word "HAT" in capital letters on Base Ten Block Grid Paper. (Be sure to darken the grid lines that fall within the letter outlines so that students cannot see them.) Make and distribute copies.

- Tell students that you want to find out which letter has the greatest area. Ask them to estimate the number of Units that they would need to cover each letter exactly. Record several estimates for each letter.

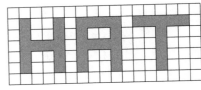

- Have students cover their letters with Units, connecting side up. Ask students to tell which letter has the greatest area and why.

- Distribute a copy of the Student Activity Sheet (page 37) to each student and review the directions as a class. Have students work in pairs.

 **Thinking and Sharing**

Discuss one floor plan at a time and invite students to tell how they estimated its size. Ask pairs to share how they decided which blocks to use to find the actual size. As students discuss their results, make a two-column list for each floor plan, recording students' estimates for the floor plan in one column and the actual size of the plan in the other.

Use prompts like these to promote class discussion:

- On what did you base your estimate?
- What method did you use for comparing the floor plans?
- Did you find any shortcuts for using the blocks? Explain.
- Did you ever think that you could tell the actual size of a floor plan without measuring it? How could you tell?

Going Further

Establish that the *area* of a region is the amount of surface the region covers. Area is measured in square units. The area of one face of a Unit block measures 1 square centimeter (1 cm²). Have students create their own school floor plan by first arranging blocks on grid paper (connecting side up) to form a "school" and then tracing around them. Each student should find the area of his or her floor plan and record it on another piece of paper as a number of square centimeters. Then have students exchange grid papers and use blocks to find the area of one another's floor plans.

SCHOOL SIZES

Which school floor plan is the biggest? Which is the smallest?

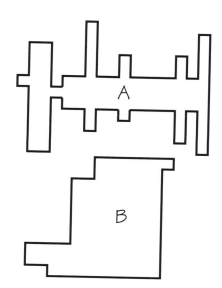

- Work with a partner and school floor plans that look like these.

- Which floor plan do you think has the greater area? Estimate.

- Use Rods and Units to find the exact size of one of the floor plans. Trade blocks when necessary. Record the exact size.

- Find and record the size of the other floor plan.

- How good were your estimates?

MODELING MULTIPLICATION

Objectives

- Reinforce understanding of the concept of area
- Identify small rectangles contained in larger rectangles
- Determine the area of a rectangle as the sum of the areas of smaller rectangles

Materials

- Interlox Base Ten Blocks, one set per student
- Crayons, four different colors per student
- Copy of Student Activity Sheet (page 39), one per student
- Base Ten Block Grid Paper (page 61), one sheet per student
- Multiplication Spinner (page 64), one per group
- Overhead Base Ten Blocks and/or Base Ten Block Grid Paper transparency (optional)

NCTM Curriculum Strands

Number & Operations
Measurement

 **Overview**

Students use Interlox Base Ten Blocks to build rectangular arrays that model the multiplication of two two-digit numbers.

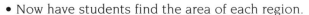 **Introducing the Activity**

- Display a Base Ten Flat and describe it as an "array" formed by rows and columns of squares.
- Call on a volunteer to explain how this array can be used to find the total number of squares in 10 rows of 10 columns.
- Use Interlox Base Ten Blocks to display a 12 × 13 array. Establish that the array is in the form of a rectangle with *dimensions* of 12 and 13.
- Ask students to identify four smaller, same-block rectangular regions within the 12 × 13 rectangle. Have them use crayons of four colors to record these regions on grid paper.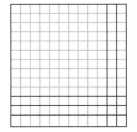
- Now have students find the area of each region.
- Elicit that the sum of the areas of the four smaller regions is equivalent to the area of the 12 × 13 rectangle.
- Distribute a copy of the Student Activity Sheet (page 39) to each student and review the directions as a class. Have students work in small groups.

 **Thinking and Sharing**

Encourage class discussion about the groups' rectangles. Have groups decide how they recorded their work and invite comparisons.

Use prompts like these to promote class discussion:

- How did you estimate the area of a big rectangle?
- What smaller rectangles did you find within a big rectangle?
- How did knowing the areas of smaller rectangles help you find the area of a big rectangle?
- How does this activity help explain why we can multiply like this to find the area of a rectangle? (Write the following on the board.)

$$\begin{array}{r} 43 \\ \times\ 22 \\ \hline \end{array}$$

 **Going Further**

Have a group put all the blocks together to make one huge rectangle, identify four smaller rectangular regions within it, and then estimate and determine its area.

MODELING MULTIPLICATION

How can you use Interlox Base Ten Blocks to model multiplication?

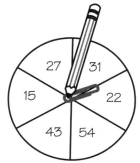

- Work with a group. Decide who will be first to spin the spinner.

- When it is your turn, spin twice. Record the numbers. Think of them as the dimensions of a rectangle.

- Build a rectangle for your dimensions with the least number of Flats, Rods, and Units possible.

- Estimate the area of your rectangle. Record your estimate.

- Now look for four smaller, same-block rectangles within your big rectangle. You may move the blocks apart slightly to show the smaller rectangles.

- Use the smaller rectangles to help you find the area of the big rectangle. Record your work.

- Keep on spinning, recording dimensions, and building rectangles until you are sure you have found the area of all the pairs of dimensions possible.

- Decide on a way to record your work.

- Leave your last rectangle where everyone can see it.

APPROXIMATING AREA

Objectives

- Estimate area
- Apply knowledge about finding the area of polygons
- Find the area of irregular shapes

Materials

- Interlox Base Ten Blocks, one set per pair
- Drawing paper, one sheet per student
- Construction paper, two large sheets per pair
- Stopwatch or clock with second hand
- Copy of Student Activity Sheet (page 41), one per student
- Base Ten Block Grid Paper (page 61), one sheet per student
- Overhead Base Ten Blocks (optional)

NCTM Curriculum Strands

Measurement
Geometry
Number & Operations

Overview

Students use Interlox Base Ten Blocks to form an irregular shape and then devise ways to find the area of this shape.

Introducing the Activity

- Tell students to place one hand flat on a sheet of drawing paper with fingers held close together. Have them trace around their hand.
- Now tell students to use Interlox Base Ten Blocks to find the area of their tracing.
- Confirm that the area cannot be measured exactly with blocks because the blocks have straight sides and square corners and the tracings have curved lines and no square corners.
- Call for students' results and list them on the board. Elicit that because the measuring can't be precise, all answers are approximations.
- Distribute a copy of the Student Activity Sheet (page 41) to each student and review the directions as a class. Have students work in pairs.

Thinking and Sharing

Remind students to make sure that the estimated area and actual area appear on each of their shapes. Post several pairs' shapes.

Use prompts like these to promote class discussion:

- How did you estimate the area of your shape?
- How did you try to find the actual area of the shape? Why did you choose this way?
- Was your estimate close to the actual area? Explain.
- How does the shape of an outline affect finding its area?

Going Further

Ask students to find the surface area—the sum of the area of all six surfaces—of a Base Ten Cube. Then have them use blocks to find the approximate surface area of another three-dimensional object with polygonal sides, such as a thick book.

APPROXIMATING AREA

How can you use Interlox Base Ten Blocks to find the area of an irregular shape?

- Work with a partner. Get one sheet of construction paper.
- Each of you take a handful of Units and then toss them onto the paper.
- Hold the paper steady as you draw an outline around your scattered Units.
- Slide the Units off the paper. Look at the shape you have drawn.
- Use blocks to estimate the area of the shape. You have just 30 seconds to do this. Record your estimate next to the shape.
- Now figure out how to use blocks to find the actual area of the shape as closely as possible. Record this actual area next to the estimated area on the shape.

A PROBLEM OF PERIMETER

Objectives

- Strengthen understanding of the concept of perimeter
- Discover that shapes with the same area do not necessarily have the same perimeter
- Recognize how the compactness of a shape affects its perimeter

Materials

- Interlox Base Ten Blocks, one or more sets per group
- Copy of the Student Activity Sheet (page 43), one per student
- Base Ten Block Grid Paper (page 61), several sheets per group
- Overhead Base Ten Blocks and/or Base Ten Block Grid Paper transparency (optional)
- Tape, one roll per group

NCTM Curriculum Strands

Geometry
Number & Operations
Measurement

Overview

Students use blocks to create a variety of shapes with a given value (area). Then they find and compare the perimeters of their shapes.

Introducing the Activity

- Make this arrangement with 4 Rods and 4 Units and have students copy it.
- Elicit that the value of the Rods is 40 and the value of the Units is 4, so the total value of the shape is 44.
- Then arrange the blocks to form a single L-shape.
- Have students do the same with their blocks.
- Establish that the *perimeter* of a shape is the distance around it.
- Review the fact that each Unit block measures 1 cm on a side.
- Have students find the perimeter of the shape. Call on several volunteers to explain how they determined that measurement.
- Distribute a copy of the Student Activity Sheet (page 43) to each student and review the directions as a class. Have students work in pairs.

Thinking and Sharing

Have students tell what they discovered about the perimeters of their shapes. Post the student recording with the shortest perimeter on the left side of the board and the one with the longest perimeter on the right. Have pairs post their shapes, in between, according to perimeter length.

Use prompts like these to promote class discussion:

- How did your shapes differ? How were they alike?
- Did the blocks you chose to model 258 affect your results? Explain.
- How did you predict the perimeter of each of your shapes?
- Did you make different kinds of predictions after you had made a few shapes?
- How can you explain the differences in the perimeters of the shapes that have the same value?
- What kinds of shapes have the shortest perimeters? What kinds have the longest?

Going Further

Challenge pairs to make several shapes, each with a perimeter of 258 units. Have them find and compare the values of these shapes with the same perimeter.

A PROBLEM OF PERIMETER

What can you predict about the perimeter of different shapes that have the same value?

- Work with a partner. Take any combination of Interlox Base Ten Blocks whose total value equals 258.

- Use all your blocks to form any flat shape. Your shape should be no higher than 1 centimeter. Your shape should not have any empty spaces that are completely surrounded by blocks.

- Record your shape on grid paper. (You may need to tape some sheets of grid paper together to do this.) Find and record the perimeter of your shape.

- Now use the same blocks to make a different shape. Predict whether or not the perimeter of this shape is the same as the perimeter of your first shape.

- Record this shape and find its perimeter. How good was your prediction?

- Make more shapes from these same blocks. Continue predicting the perimeter of each shape, recording the shape and your estimate, and then finding the shape's perimeter.

- Be ready to talk about your predictions and to tell how to compare the perimeters of shapes with the same value.

MAKING AND WRITING DECIMALS

Objectives
- Model decimal amounts
- Compare the relative values of tenths and hundredths
- Add decimal amounts
- Develop strategic thinking skills

Materials
- Interlox Base Ten Blocks, two sets per group
- Copy of Student Activity Sheet (page 45), one per student

NCTM Curriculum Strands
Number & Operations

Overview

In this game for two or four players, students collect blocks with decimal values in an effort to be the first to reach a numerical goal.

Introducing the Activity

- Provide small groups with Flats, Rods, and Units. Have each group line up 10 Rods on a Flat and 10 Units on one of the Rods.
- Hold up a Flat and tell students to pretend that the Flat has the value of one whole (1).
- Elicit that since a Flat is made up of 10 Rods, each Rod has a value of one-tenth (0.1); similarly, since a Rod is made up of 10 Units, each Unit has a value of one-tenth of one-tenth, or one-hundredth (0.01).
- Distribute a copy of the Student Activity Sheet (page 45) to each student. Go over the game rules for Making and Writing Decimals.
- Invite two volunteers to play a few rounds of the game with you as the rest of the class keeps score.

Thinking and Sharing

Invite students to talk about their games and describe some of the thinking they did.

Use prompts like these to promote class discussion:
- When did you decide to add Rods instead of Units? When did you decide to add Units instead of Rods? Explain.
- Do you think that you would have played differently if there were a different number of players? Explain.
- Were you able to predict the winner before the game ended? If so, at what point were you able to predict?
- If you could change the rules of this game, what changes would you make?

Going Further

Have students play the game again, this time assigning the value of 1 to a Cube. Be sure that students understand how this affects the relative values of each of the other kinds of blocks; then allow them to change the game rules to suit this game.

MAKING AND WRITING DECIMALS

Play Making and Writing Decimals! Here are the rules:

- This is a game for two or four players. The object is to build a collection of Interlox Base Ten Blocks whose value matches the "goal." The goal will be a collection of blocks with a decimal value because, in this game:

  Flats = 1 (a whole)

  Rods = 0.1 (a tenth)

  Units = 0.01 (a hundredth)

- Each player makes a collection of Flats, Rods, and Units.
- The group finds the value of each collection.
- The collection with the greatest value becomes the goal. Each player makes a copy of the collection with the least value and uses it as a "starting number."
- Players decide who will go first. On each turn, a player adds certain blocks to his or her own starting number and then finds and records the new value of the collection. A player may add 1 Rod or 2 Rods, or 1 Unit or 2 Units.
- Whoever is the first to collect blocks with a value that matches the goal number exactly wins the game.

DECIMAL MIRRORS

Objectives

- Assign decimal values to Interlox Base Ten Blocks
- Use blocks to model decimal amounts
- Add, subtract, and compare decimal amounts

Materials

- Interlox Base Ten Blocks, one set per pair
- Large books to use as barriers
- Copy of Student Activity Sheet (page 47), one per student
- Place Value Mat (page 54), one per student

NCTM Curriculum Strands

Number & Operations

Overview

Students secretly build collections of blocks that represent decimal amounts. Then they try to "mirror" each other's collections.

Introducing the Activity

- Out of students' sight, arrange 4 Flats, 7 Rods, and 6 Units on a place value mat. Cover the blocks with another mat and keep them hidden.
- Explain that the blocks can be used to model fraction amounts. Hold up a Flat. Tell students to imagine that this block, made up of 100 units, has a value of 1.
- Elicit that if a Flat is worth 1, then a Unit is worth $\frac{1}{100}$. Write the decimal form of one-hundredth, 0.01, on the board.
- Also elicit that if a Flat is worth 1, then a Rod is worth $\frac{10}{100}$, or $\frac{1}{10}$. Write this as 0.1.
- Tell students that you have hidden a collection of blocks worth 4.76.
- Ask them to try to duplicate your collection using the least number of blocks possible.
- Reveal your blocks. Ask students to check their blocks to see if they match yours. (Tell anyone whose collection does not match yours to determine which blocks to add or subtract to make the collection "mirror" yours.)
- Distribute a copy of the Student Activity Sheet (page 47) to each student and review the directions as a class. Have students work in pairs.

Thinking and Sharing

Encourage pairs to walk around the room to look at other pairs' "mirror" collections. Have them compare the decimal values of the blocks on each pair of place value mats.

Use prompts like these to promote class discussion:

- What was easy about this activity? What was difficult? Explain.
- What was the largest collection you "mirrored"? The smallest?
- After you added and subtracted, did your two collections always match? Explain.
- What did you do if you found that your collections did not match?
- How do you think you could get better at mirroring block collections?

Going Further

Have students repeat the activity by naming amounts that they multiply or divide instead of add or subtract.

DECIMAL MIRRORS

How can you use Interlox Base Ten Blocks to "mirror" decimal amounts?

- Work with a partner. Decide who will be first to model an amount.
- Whoever goes first secretly models a decimal amount on a place value mat using Flats, Rods, and Units. (Remember: Flat = 1; Rod = 0.1; and Unit = 0.01)

Then this partner records the value of the block collection and says the value aloud.

- The other partner also records the amount and then secretly tries to "mirror" it on another place value mat.
- Now partners take turns naming amounts to add or to subtract from their collections. For example:

> If a partner says, "Add two and three-tenths," then both partners add blocks worth 2.3 to their mat. Each writes the new total value of his or her collection.
>
> or
>
> If a partner says, "Subtract forty-two hundredths," then both partners take blocks worth 0.42 off their mat. They each write the new total value of their collection.

- After each partner has had three turns, partners display and compare their collections. If the collections don't match, partners find the difference in the values and try to figure out why they don't match.
- Repeat the activity several times.
- Leave your last collections out for everyone to see.

Interlox™ Base Ten Blocks Activity Guide

FAIR SHARES

Objectives

- Build an understanding of division
- Determine why division sometimes involves a remainder
- Make sense of the standard division algorithm

Materials

- Interlox Base Ten Blocks (Flats, Rods, and Units), two or three sets per group
- Interlox Base Ten Blocks Cube, one per group
- Copy of Student Activity Sheet (page 49), one per student
- Overhead Base Ten Blocks (optional)

NCTM Curriculum Strands

Number & Operations

Overview

Students use Interlox Base Ten Blocks to model division with one-digit divisors and three- and four-digit dividends.

Introducing the Activity

- Display 1 Flat, 2 Rods, and 3 Units. Have each student do the same.
- Ask students to show how they could each share their blocks equally with two other people.
- Elicit that trading the Flat for 10 Rods would make a total of 12 Rods. Then, 12 Rods and 3 Units could be distributed equally among three students, with each getting 4 Rods and 1 Unit. (Note: If not enough Rods are available for each student to trade a Flat for 10 Rods, have students work in groups of three.)
- Ask volunteers to describe possible ways of recording what they modeled.
- Distribute a copy of the Student Activity Sheet (page 49) to each student and review the directions as a class. Have students work in groups of three to six.

Thinking and Sharing

Invite groups to display their recordings and talk about how they worked.

Use prompts like these to promote class discussion:

- What was the value of your first collection?
- How did you go about creating fair shares?
- How did you record your work? Why did you choose this method?
- After you made the shares as fair as possible, did you have any blocks left over? If so, what did you do with the remainder?
- How did the value of a fair share change when someone in the group did not take a share?
- How could you use some of these symbols to record fair shares and remainders? (Write the following on the board: ÷, ‾)‾‾‾ , R.)
- How did including a Cube in your activity change the activity?

Going Further

- Have students create collections that would yield fair shares of a predetermined value. You might ask, for example, "What collection of blocks would give your group fair shares, each with a value of 50 with no remainder? With a value of 23 with no remainder? With a value of 19 with 3 as a remainder?"

FAIR SHARES

How can you make fair shares of an Interlox Base Ten Block collection?

- Work in a group of 3–6. Make a big collection of blocks using any combination of Flats, Rods, and Units.

- Estimate what the value of each share would be if you share your collection fairly. Record your estimate.

- Share the collection so everyone in the group gets blocks with the same value.

- Find the actual value of each share. Record it.

- Now, combine all the blocks. Have one member of the group make fair shares for everyone except for himself or herself. Estimate the value of each of these fair shares. Then share the blocks and record the actual value of each share.

- Combine the blocks again, but this time include a Cube with a value of 1,000.

- Estimate the value of each fair share of this last collection for everyone in the group. Make the fair shares and record all your work.

DOUBLE THE DIMENSIONS

Objectives

- Increase spatial visualization skills
- Determine and compare volume and surface area
- Predict the volume and surface area of a "doubled" structure

Materials

- Interlox Base Ten Blocks (Flats, Rods, and Units), two sets per pair
- Copy of Student Activity Sheet (page 51), one per student
- Interlox Base Ten Blocks Cubes, three or more per pair (optional)

NCTM Curriculum Strands

Number & Operations
Measurement

Overview

Students use blocks to design and build structures. They determine the volume and surface area of their structures and then predict how these will change when they "double" their structures.

Introducing the Activity

- Have each student examine a Rod as you ask the class to determine its volume.
- Elicit that since volume can be represented by the number of cubic centimeters that make up a solid figure, the volume of a Rod is 10 cm³.
- Challenge students to find the surface area of the Rod.
- Be sure students understand that since surface area is the total number of square units that completely cover the outside of a shape, the surface area of a Rod is 42 cm².
- Now have each student examine a Flat and determine its volume and surface area.
- Establish that the volume of a Flat is 100 cm³ and that the surface area is 240 cm².
- Put a Flat and a Rod together in any way so that at least 1 square centimeter of each touches the other. Identify this block arrangement as a "structure."
- Lead students to talk about how they could find the volume and surface area of this structure.
- Distribute a copy of the Student Activity Sheet (page 51) to each student and review the directions as a class. Have students work in pairs.

Thinking and Sharing

Allow students to examine the structures built by various pairs, telling them to compare each first structure with its doubled version.

Use prompts like these to promote class discussion:

- How did you go about doubling your first structure?
- What did you do to find volume? What did you do to find surface area?
- Did you find any surprises when you doubled a structure? Explain.
- What changes in volume and surface area did you notice between a first structure and a doubled structure?
- Which way of doubling a structure do you think was best? Explain.

Going Further

Have students describe why architects or designers might need to know the volume and/or surface area of a structure or container.

DOUBLE THE DIMENSIONS

How can you use Interlox Base Ten Blocks to determine how the volume and surface area of a structure change when you double its dimensions?

- Work with a partner. Each of you build a structure using any blocks according to these rules:

  - All blocks must either lie down flat or stand up on end. They may not lean.
  - Each block must touch another block by at least 1 square centimeter.

- Work together to find the volume and the surface area of each of your structures. Remember: *Volume* is the number of cubic units that make up a structure. *Surface area* is the number of square units that completely cover a structure. Here are two examples:

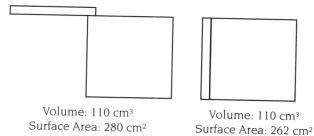

Volume: 110 cm³
Surface Area: 280 cm²

Volume: 110 cm³
Surface Area: 262 cm²

- Now, think about how you can double your first structures. Predict what the volume and surface area of each doubled structure would be.

- Without taking your first structures apart, build new structures with doubled dimensions. Find and record the volume and surface area of each doubled structure.

- Be ready to tell how you doubled your structures and how the new dimensions compare to the old ones.

PAVING PLACES

Objectives

- Estimate and determine area
- Investigate percent spatially
- Use percent to compute costs

Materials

- Interlox Base Ten Blocks, one set per pair
- Copy of Student Activity Sheet (page 53), one per student
- Base Ten Block Grid Paper (page 61), several sheets per pair
- Calculators (optional)

NCTM Curriculum Strands

Number & Operations
Measurement
Geometry

Overview

Students use Interlox Base Ten Blocks to "pave," or completely tile, a desktop or other workspace. Students determine which kinds of blocks to use—according to the monetary values that have been assigned to each—as they try to pave their workspaces at the least possible "cost."

Introducing the Activity

- Call on a volunteer to point out a classroom object that could have a cost of $1.00.
- Tell students to pretend that the object did cost $1.00, but that now it is "on sale" at a 10% discount. Ask students how much the object would cost now.
- Establish that the sale price is $.90. Elicit that this is because $1.00 represents 100 cents and that 10% of 100 cents is represented by the fraction $\frac{10}{100}$, or $\frac{1}{10}$, and that one-tenth of 100 is 10.
- Now tell students to pretend that the same object will be on sale tomorrow at a 20% discount. Ask students to determine how much the object will cost tomorrow.
- Distribute a copy of the Student Activity Sheet (page 53) to each student and review the directions as a class. Have students work in pairs.

Thinking and Sharing

Give pairs the opportunity to describe how they did their work. Have students gather around each pair's workspace as they discuss how it was paved.

Use prompts like these to promote class discussion:

- What is the size of your workspace in square units?
- How did you estimate the cost of paving your workspace with Unit pavers only?
- How much of a savings would you have by paving using Flats and Rods instead of Units alone?
- How can you explain the difference in costs for paving workspaces of the same size?
- Would it cost twice as much to pave a particular workspace twice as big as yours? Explain.

Going Further

- Ask students to estimate the cost of paving the entire classroom, assuming the same prices as those used or the activity.
- Have students describe how they could pave their workspaces in a decorative way. Tell them to sketch a design for the blocks and include an estimate of what it would cost for their decorative paving.

PAVING PLACES

How can you use Interlox Base Ten Blocks to "pave" your workspace at the least possible cost?

- Work with a partner. Imagine that Interlox Base Ten Blocks are paving stones, or "pavers." Decide on a workspace that you can pave with these pavers.

- Think: If each Unit paver costs $3.00, what would be the cost of each Rod paver? What would be the cost of each Flat paver?

- Estimate what it would cost to pave your workspace if you used only Unit pavers. Record your estimate.

Here's some good news—Rods and Flats are on sale!

    SALE PRICES

    10% off on Rods

    20% of on Flats

- Now figure out how to pave your workspace the least costly way, using any combinations of pavers. Record your work.

- Be ready to explain how you decided to pave your workspace.

PLACE VALUE MAT

FLATS (hundreds)	RODS (tens)	UNITS (ones)

©ETA/Cuisenaire®

UNITS/RODS SPINNER

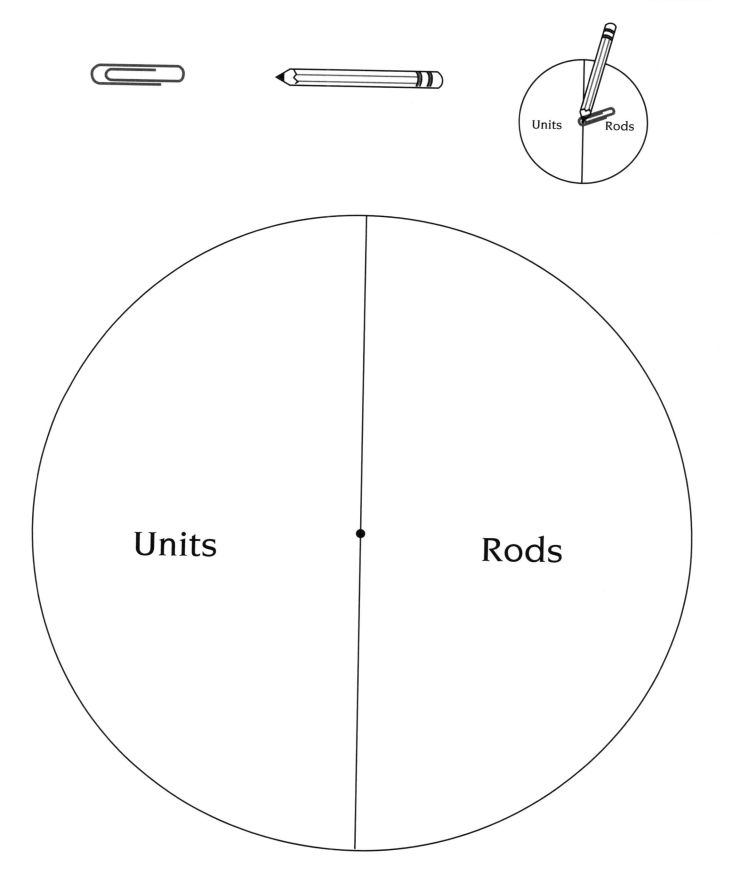

SUM IT UP!

Put your blocks here.

Your Sum: _____

1.
_____ + _____ = _____

2.
_____ + _____ = _____

3.
_____ + _____ = _____

4.
_____ + _____ = _____

5.
_____ + _____ = _____

6.
_____ + _____ = _____

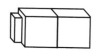

WHAT'S THE DIFFERENCE? GAME BOARD

START

3	5	1	8	0	2

					7
					4

4	7	2	3	6	1

0
5
8

FINISH

1	6	2	9	5

ONE OR TWO SPINNER

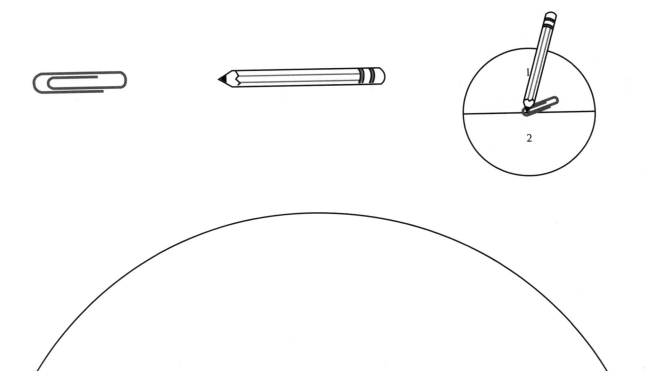

1

2

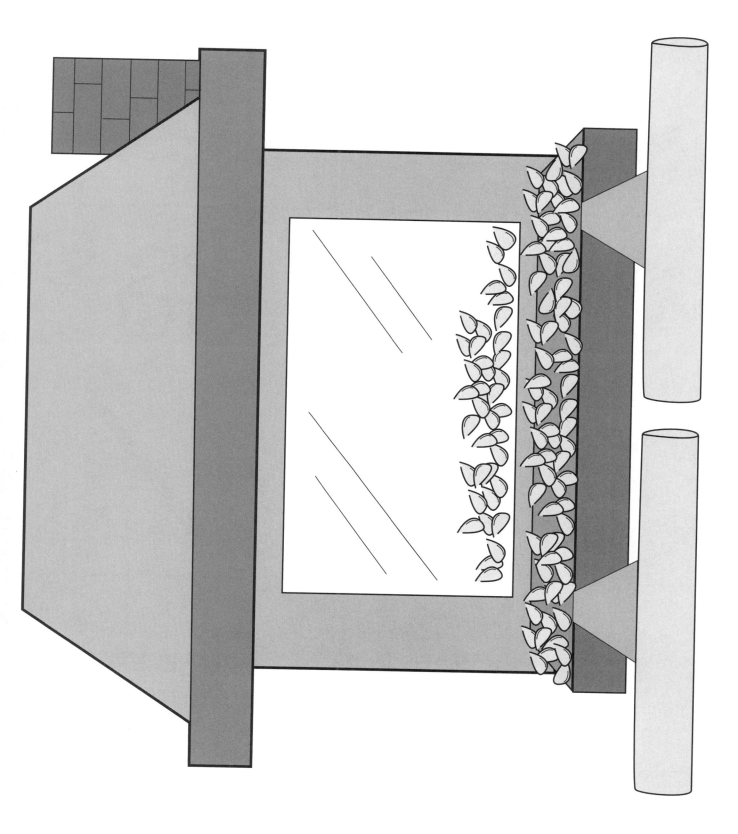

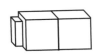
WHAT WILL YOU BUY?

$3.00

$7.49

$5.95

$1.25

$8.20

$6.38

$10.00

Music CD

$4.50

$2.41

$2.75

28.03

$9.10

$3.66

Video

Interlox™ Base Ten Blocks Activity Guide

BASE TEN BLOCK GRID PAPER

PUT-IN-PLACE MAT

Round	RODS	UNITS
1		
2		
3		
4		
5		
	TOTAL ⟶	

SCHOOL FLOOR PLANS

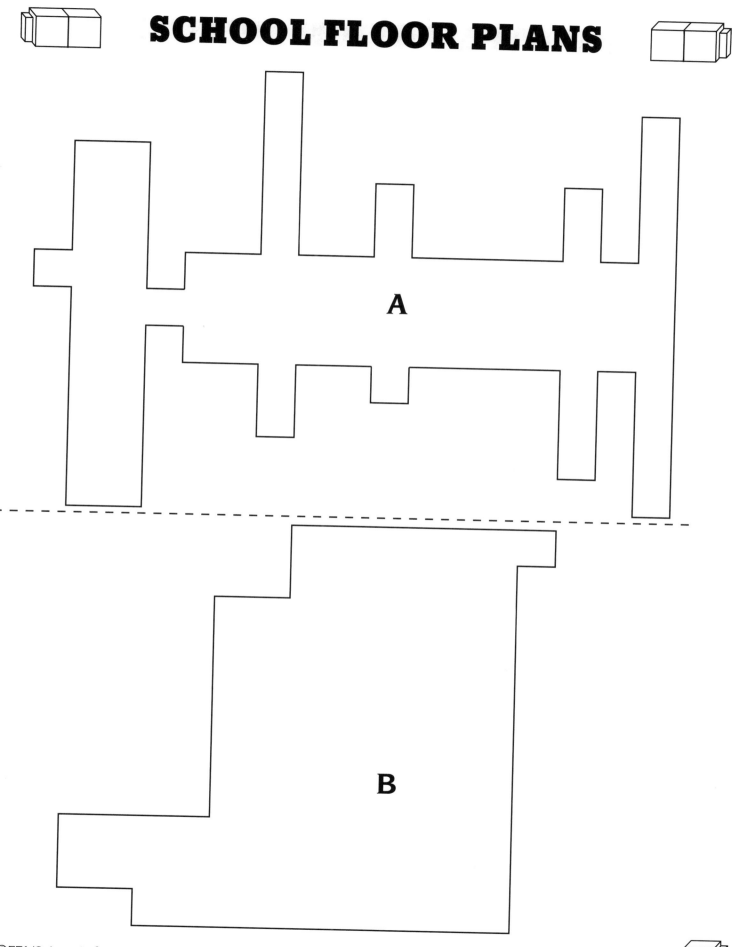

MULTIPLICATION SPINNER

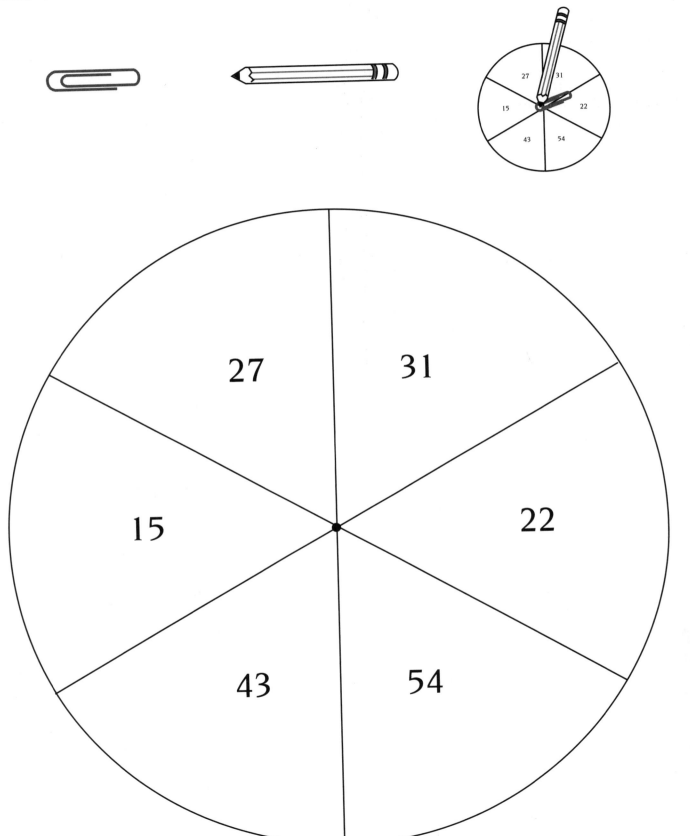